Christopher Columbus, Admiral of the Unknown Sea

by
Richard P. Emanuel

Cornelsen

Christopher Columbus, Admiral of the Unknown Sea

von
Richard P. Emanuel

Verlagsredaktion
Susanne Döpper

Technische Umsetzung
Harald Kertz

Grafik
Gabriele Heinisch, Berlin

Bildquellen
s. Verzeichnis auf S. 47

1. Auflage 1991

Druck: Adolph Fürst & Sohn, Berlin

ISBN: 3-464-05338-5
Vertrieb: Cornelsen Verlagsgesellschaft, Bielefeld
Bestellnummer 53385

Contents

Chapter One
The great enterprise

Columbus' years in Genoa

The story of the man who found America began in a city by the sea. Christopher Columbus was born in the Mediterranean Sea port of Genoa, Italy, in the year 1451. At that time Genoa was a busy center of trade, as it is today. Sailing ships came and went and carried things of great worth from distant lands. Columbus was fascinated by the sea when he was a boy. By the time he was 14 years old, he had begun to sail in the waters around Genoa.

Christopher was the oldest child in his family, or at least the oldest who survived. He had one sister and three younger brothers; two of them later journeyed in America. Columbus' father was a master weaver, and both of his grandfathers were weavers, too. Columbus worked in his father's business when he was young and probably had very little time for school. When he became older, he worked on sailing ships in the Mediterranean Sea as often as he could.

Columbus' first adventure at sea happened in the summer of 1476. He was a young sailor in a fleet of ships that carried things from Genoa to several Atlantic Ocean ports. The fleet had sailed out of the Mediterranean Sea and was several kilometers away from the southern coast of Portugal when it was attacked by Portuguese and French warships. The battle lasted all day, and when it was over, seven ships had sunk and hundreds of men were dead. The ship Columbus was on was one of those that had sunk. He was hurt, but he held onto a floating piece of wood and was able to swim ten kilometers to land. The people of the town where he landed were kind to him. When he was healthy enough to travel again, they sent him to Lisbon, where his brother, Bartholomew, had recently moved.

Columbus' years in Portugal

Columbus was lucky that he had landed in Portugal. It had the best sailing technology in Europe in the late fifteenth century. Portuguese ships sailed from Iceland in the north to the coast of Africa in the south. Columbus thought he could learn a lot by staying in Portugal. Altogether he spent nine years there. With his brother, Bartholomew, he made and sold charts of the sea. He also sailed, both for adventure and to make money. Probably in late 1479, Columbus married the daughter of an important Portuguese family. The next year he and his wife had a son, Diego.

During the years when he lived in Portugal, Columbus learned much about sailing and the sea. He also sailed from Lisbon to ports in Ireland and Iceland where people told stories about Viking journeys to lands far to the west. For although this knowledge was later almost forgotten, it was the Vikings who discovered America long before Columbus.

The first Europeans who reached America

Six hundred years before Columbus sailed to America — longer before Columbus' journey than his journey was before today — a strong people pushed west from northern Europe in small boats across the sea to Iceland. The Vikings built a colony in Iceland and pushed farther west to Greenland, where they built a smaller colony about the year 986. Legend says that a Viking ship was blown off course as it sailed to the new colony, and became lost for many days in thick fog. When the fog cleared, the sailors saw a new coast with a great forest, but it was not Greenland. They knew that the wind had blown them to the southwest, so they sailed northeast and at last landed in Greenland, where they told people what had happened.

Sixteen years later, in 1002, a Viking called Leif Erickson, whose father had established the Greenland colony, decided to look for the strange land which he had heard about as a boy. Leif sailed southwest from Greenland to a place he named Vinland because of the grapes that grew there. He and his men spent the winter in Vinland, now a part of Canada called Newfoundland. They returned home with news of their adventure, and soon other Vikings sailed to build houses and farms in Vinland. We know that at least part of the legend is true because in the 1960s, the ruins of Viking houses were found on Newfoundland.

From Vinland the Vikings explored the coast of what is now Canada. People have long argued about how far they traveled from their colony. There is reason to believe that they reached as far south as what is now the northeastern United States. It was very difficult to keep ties between Vinland, Greenland, and other Viking lands, even with the best ships of the eleventh century. Because of this and because of attacks from Native Americans, the Viking colony in Vinland died out after about 20 years. Knowledge of this land, thousands of kilometers across the sea from Europe, was kept alive only in legend.

Did the young Columbus hear the Vinland legend when he sailed to Iceland in 1477? Some writers believe that he did. Others say he probably did not because he did not speak the language of Iceland. The truth is, no one knows whether or not he heard the story, but if he did, he never wrote about it. It is possible that he heard pieces of the legend, but that stories of northern forests and fish did not interest him. Like most Europeans of his time, Columbus was much more interested in the rich countries in Asia.

A new route to Asia

In the fifteenth century, many Asian spices came to Europe through India and across Arab lands to the Mediterranean Sea. Things from Asia were very expensive because it was a long and often dangerous journey. Many people were needed to bring the spices and other things to Europe, and each person wanted money for his work. Anyone who could find a simpler way to bring things from Asia would surely get rich.

In addition, the known route to India was controled by Muslims. Over the centuries Muslims had moved from Arabia up to Turkey in the north and across Africa and into Spain in the south. As the European Christians did not want to be part of a Muslim empire and its Muslim religion, they had tried to fight the Muslims. In the time of Columbus, Muslims were being pushed out of Spain, which had just been united when King Ferdinand and Queen Isabella were married. However, the Muslims still had control of the spice trade. What the Christian Europeans needed was a route to the rich ports of Asia that did not go through Arabia.

Portugal led the way during the fifteenth century as Europeans looked for a sea route to Asia. Ships from Portugal pushed south along the coast of Africa because they hoped to find a route around that continent to India. In 1482, they established a colony in Africa, where they traded for gold and later for slaves. Portuguese ships also discovered and settled several groups of islands in the Atlantic Ocean. The most important of these were the Azores.

As Europeans sailed farther south and west into the Atlantic Ocean, their knowledge of geography grew. But their world was still not very different from the world that the Greeks of old had known. They knew about Europe, Africa, and Asia, of course, three great continents that touched the Mediterranean Sea. They believed that all of this — all the known world — was surrounded by one great ocean. There were islands in the ocean, and some of them were large, but few people imagined that unknown continents waited to be discovered.

When Columbus was a boy in Genoa, he must have heard many strange stories about the ocean. Superstitious people believed that there were monsters ready to destroy ships that sailed too far from land. People thought that the world was round, but they wondered what held it up underneath. They thought if a ship sailed too far down the side of the earth, near the equator, it might fall off. And because the weather was cold in the north and hotter farther south, they thought it would be so hot near the equator that no one could survive. When Portuguese ships at last sailed south of the equator as they looked for a route around Africa, some of these ideas were finally shown to be wrong. But stories of sea monsters and other superstitions lived on for many more years.

No one knows when Columbus first got the idea that he could sail west to reach the rich ports of Asia. Perhaps he got the idea during one of his earlier ocean journeys to Iceland, the Azores or the Portuguese colony in Africa. Perhaps he thought of it as he drew sea charts with Bartholomew. Perhaps a forgotten sea captain suggested it while he talked with Columbus in a Lisbon pub. All we know is that, in 1484, Columbus suggested to the King of Portugal a westward journey to Asia. The King asked his experts what they thought, but they were more interested in an African route to "the Indies", as they called India and the spice islands of Asia. The King said no to Columbus.
For the next eight years, Columbus worked very hard to get the money he needed for what he called "the great enterprise of the Indies". Soon after the King refused his idea, Columbus' wife died and he decided to leave Portugal. He sailed to Spain with his five-year old son, Diego, and began to talk about his idea with anyone who would listen.

Columbus asks the Spanish King and Queen for help

In Spain Columbus met a rich owner of ships who was almost ready to pay for his journey to the Indies, but only if Queen Isabella gave her permission. The Queen thought that such an important journey should be made on behalf of the King and Queen, if it should be made at all. So in May 1486, Columbus appeared before Queen Isabella and King Ferdinand to describe the journey and to ask for their help. Isabella was interested in Columbus' idea. She liked the confident and excited way he talked about his plans. But she and Ferdinand had to spend most of their money to push the last Muslims out of Spain. Before she was ready to give Columbus the money he wanted, she asked a group of experts for their opinions. When the experts met at the end of 1486, they could not agree on what they should tell the Queen. So Columbus waited and waited for a decision from the Spanish experts and from the King and Queen.

One reason the experts could not agree about Columbus' idea was because they did not agree about how far west he would have to sail. Columbus believed that China was 6,600 kilometers west of Europe, a distance that he could sail in about six weeks. Japan was closer and could be reached by ship in less than a month, he thought. Many experts did not believe that Asia was so close, and they were right. Japan is about 20,000 kilometers west of Europe, a distance that would have taken Columbus more than four months to sail. But there was something important that the experts did not know, and it was something Columbus did not know either: If a ship sailed west from Europe for about six weeks, it would hit, not Asia, but America.

Month after month went by while Columbus waited to hear from the King and Queen of Spain. He talked with friends and sea captains, he read books and he became impatient. During this time, he fell in love with a Spanish woman. He never married her, but in 1488 she gave birth to Ferdinand Columbus, his second son. Ferdinand sailed with his father on his last journey to America, and later wrote a book about his father.

Columbus was not happy as he waited in Spain. He decided to write to the King of Portugal to ask if he could talk with him again about his enterprise. He traveled to Lisbon, where his brother, Bartholomew, still made sea charts. He was with his brother in December 1488, when a Portuguese ship returned to Lisbon with news that it had sailed around the southern tip of Africa, almost to India. When he heard this news, the King of Portugal lost any interest he had in the crazy idea of Columbus to sail westward to Asia.

The Columbus brothers were discouraged, but they were not ready to quit, so they made another plan. Christopher returned to Spain, where he waited for the experts to advise the Queen. Bartholomew traveled to England and France to see if those countries were interested in their journey. Another year and a half went by before the experts in Spain finally decided. Their answer was no, but the Queen told Columbus to ask her again when the war against the Muslims had ended.

Another year went by before the war ended and Columbus talked to the Queen again. Her experts still advised her to say no to him, and in January 1492, she did. Columbus was terribly discouraged. He had tried for eight long years to find the money he needed to make his journey. Sadly he prepared to leave Spain.

What happened next seemed like a wonder to Columbus. He left the castle, and as he traveled on the road, a messenger reached him and asked him to return. The King and Queen had decided that they would pay for his journey after all. Their answer was "Yes!" Columbus needed to wait no longer for his adventures to begin.

Columbus was lucky that the King and Queen agreed to his idea when they did because other people had plans like his. In 1492 a geographer from Nuremberg named Martin Behaim built a globe that was based on ideas of the world that were like those of Columbus. The next year a friend of Behaim's wrote to the King of Portugal to ask for a ship so Behaim could sail west to Asia. But he was too late. Columbus had already returned from his first journey of discovery.

Chapter Two
Westward sail! The journey of discovery

Columbus was a very proud man. Although he had waited eight years to sail to the Indies, he discussed the conditions of his trip for another three months before he agreed to go. In the end Queen Isabella and King Ferdinand gave him everything he wanted.

Columbus was given the title of Admiral. He would become the governor of any new lands he discovered. Ten percent of any gold, jewels, spices, or other things that might be produced in the new lands would belong to Columbus and to his children after him. The King and Queen also gave him a letter for the ruler of China. The letter was supposed to help establish trade between Spain and China.

In May 1492, Columbus traveled to the port of Palos, Spain, to prepare three ships for the journey. The biggest ship was the Santa Maria and it carried the Admiral. The two smaller ships were named the Nina and the Pinta. The Nina was the fastest ship in the little fleet, and it became Columbus' favorite.

Ninety men sailed with Columbus on his journey of discovery. It took more than two months to find enough sailors who were willing to go, and to buy all the food, water, wine, and other supplies they would need. They took enough supplies to last for a year.

At last all was ready. Columbus and his men were all Catholics, and they went to church the night before they sailed. Then, early in the morning of Friday, August 3, 1492, Columbus climbed onto the Santa Maria and ordered the fleet to sail. Half an hour before the sun rose, the Nina, the Pinta, and the Santa Maria raised their anchors and floated down the river from Palos into the sea, and into history.

Before Columbus turned west, he sailed 1,200 kilometers southwest from Spain to the Canary Islands. Spain had

Columbus starting his first journey of discovery

recently taken control of the islands, and Columbus wanted to load a little more fresh water and food before the long journey into the unknown. Just a few days after they left Spain, the Pinta's steering machine broke, and a few days after that, the ship started to leak. The fleet spent four weeks in the Canaries. They repaired the Pinta and loaded fresh supplies. On September 6, the work was done. The ships raised anchors and sails and began to leave the Canaries.

Columbus was very clever to start his first crossing of the Atlantic Ocean from the Canaries instead of from Spain. The islands are farther west than Spain, of course, but they have an even more important advantage. When Columbus had sailed from Portugal to Africa as a young man, he had noticed that winds in the latitude of the Canary Islands often blew from east to west. Farther north, in the latitude of Spain, Portugal, and the Azores, winds blew more often from the west. Columbus' plan was to sail west with the wind from the Canaries, and to sail north to the latitude of the Azores and then turn east, with the wind, on his way back. This plan made use of the system of winds called the trade winds, which were very important to sailors as long as ships used sails.

Of course, the trade winds do not always blow, and when Columbus prepared to leave the Canaries, the wind was weak. The fleet sailed slowly the first few days, and Tenerife volcano, whose top is 3,600 meters above the sea, could be seen until the third day. Finally, as night fell on September 9, 1492, the wind from the east grew stronger and the Nina, the Pinta, and the Santa Maria sailed beyond the sight of land, and into an unknown sea.

We know a lot about what happened on Columbus' first crossing to America because he wrote in a journal every day. He recorded the weather, the course of the ships, how the men felt, and some of his own thoughts. Columbus was a religious man, and he believed that God guided his adventure.

Unfortunately Columbus' journal was lost after he died, but not before one of his friends wrote a summary of the journal. The summary has survived, and it is now in a museum in Spain. From this summary we can guess what was written in the Admiral's original journal.

<u>Monday, September 10th, 1492</u>   No land could be seen today. Very strong winds blew, and we sailed about 280 kilometers. I told the men we sailed only 230 kilometers because I do not want to frighten them if this becomes a long journey.

<u>Saturday, September 15th</u>   There was a wonderful fire-ball in the sky last night, probably a signal of good luck. We sailed almost 100 kilometers, but I told the sailors it was a little less than that.

<u>Sunday, September 16th</u>   Today the wind was strong, and we sailed about 180 kilometers. There were some clouds in the sky and a little rain, but the mornings have all been fair, like April mornings in southern Spain.

<u>Wednesday, September 19th</u>   The wind started to drop during the day, and we traveled only 120 kilometers. We saw two birds today of a kind which do not go very far from land. I believe there are islands around us, but I do not want to take time to look for them. If God is willing, we will look for them on the way back from the Indies. This evening we had a meeting with all three ships, and we agreed that the fleet has sailed about 2,000 kilometers west from the Canaries. This is twice as far from land as anyone has ever sailed before.

<u>Thursday, September 20th</u>   Calm wind today. We sailed only 35 kilometers. We saw more birds. A sailor caught one with his hands.

<u>Saturday, September 22nd</u>   Today the wind blew from the west for the first time since we left the Canaries, and it was a good thing. The sailors have complained. They are worried that it will be difficult to

sail back to Spain against the wind, which so often blows from the east in this sea. Today's wind from the west made them happy. We sailed 140 kilometers.

<u>Sunday, September 23rd</u> We traveled about 100 kilometers today. There were many birds, and in some places the sea was full of green plants that floated. The sailors are frightened that we will not be able to sail back to Spain. The sea was very smooth until late in the day. Then the waves grew very high, although the wind was calm, and the sailors were amazed. I told them that these waves are a signal from God, who guards our fleet and wants us to sail farther.

<u>Tuesday, September 25th</u> This morning the wind was calm, but in the afternoon it blew. I wanted to discuss where we were with the captain of the Pinta, so he sailed his ship next to the Santa Maria while we talked. We used a rope to send a chart from one ship to the other. Late in the day the Pinta's captain shouted that he saw land in the southwest! The sailors climbed high on the ropes to look, and they all agreed that it was land. They looked until the sun went down. We thanked God and I ordered the fleet to sail southwest.

<u>Wednesday, September 26th</u> Bitter disappointment! This morning we saw no land. What we saw last night was probably a dark cloud. We turned again to the west and sailed almost 150 kilometers today, but I told the men we went 115. The sea here is as smooth as a river, and the air smells sweet.

<u>Friday, September 28th</u> Calm today. We traveled a little more than 60 kilometers. The men caught fish.

<u>Saturday, September 29th</u> The winds were weak again, but the sea was smooth and the air smelled very sweet. It was a perfect day.

<u>Monday, October 1st</u> It has been 26 days since our little fleet left the Canaries. We have gone west more than 3,400 kilometers. Some

of the men are terribly worried that they will never see Spain again. Today there was heavy rain.

<u>Wednesday, October 3rd</u> We sailed 230 kilometers today. There were many plants that floated in the water, some with a kind of fruit.

<u>Thursday, October 4th</u> Today we sailed more than 300 kilometers with strong winds. A group of 40 birds flew over the fleet. A boy on the ship hit one bird with a stone.

<u>Friday, October 5th</u> The wind was strong but the sea was smooth, and we traveled 275 kilometers today. There were many flying fish, and some jumped out of the ocean and into our ships. The air smelled very sweet. Tonight the moon was full, and the sea all around us was the color of silver, and brilliant.

<u>Sunday, October 7th</u> This morning, the little Nina sailed ahead of the rest of our fleet. Everyone wants to be the first to see land. During the day the Nina raised a flag and shot a cannon, which was a signal that they had seen land. But in the evening we did not see any land, so it was another wrong report. This evening a very large group of birds flew towards the southwest, over the ships. I believe that they always sleep on land, so there must be land near. I ordered the ships to sail southwest.

<u>Tuesday, October 9th</u> The men are very worried because we have sailed so far. Before they would sail any farther, they made me promise to turn around if we do not see land within three days. Birds flew over us all night. We sailed 100 kilometers today.

<u>Wednesday, October 10th</u> The men are angry. They complained and shouted that if we don't find land within two days, they will force me to turn around! I told them we will all be rich if we find the Indies. And I told them that we will continue to sail to the west.

Thursday, October 11th We sailed 370 kilometers today. The wind was very strong, and the waves were very high. The Nina saw a green branch that floated in the water. It had red flowers. Sailors on the Pinta took a carved stick from the sea. There were no complaints today, everyone believes that land is near. When the sun went down, we thanked God, and I told the men to watch with great care tonight.

— 11 p.m., October 11th One hour ago, before the moon rose, I thought I saw a very small light in the dark sea ahead! I called a man to look and he saw it, but another man did not see it. Then I saw it again!

— 2:30 a.m., Friday, October 12th, 1492 Land! Half an hour ago a sailor on the Pinta, which was ahead of my Santa Maria, saw a white sand beach far ahead, like a ghost in the moonlight. The Pinta's captain saw it too, and shot a cannon to let us know. This time the report is true. We have all seen land a short distance away! I have ordered all three ships to slowly sail from side to side until morning when we will look for a safe place to anchor. Thank God! Our great enterprise is a success! We have sailed west, across the great ocean, to the Indies. When the sun rises in a few more hours, what wonders will we see?

Chapter Three
In the Indies — or where?

On "Discovery Island"

The morning sun on October 12, 1492, brought a wonderful sight to Christopher Columbus and his 90 tired men. They had sailed west from the Canaries for 5,700 kilometers and had seen no land for 33 days. Now they saw before them a beautiful island with dark green forests, tall palm trees, and white sand beaches, brilliant in the morning sun. It was a jewel, surrounded by clear, blue water. On the shore there were people who wore no clothes. They looked strong and healthy and had brown skin.

These were amazing things. But they were no more amazing than the things the people who lived on the island saw on that day. Three great wooden ships with huge, white sails like clouds floated around a corner of land, dropped anchors, and stopped in the water. A small boat came down from the biggest ship, and men came to the shore. They were strange men who wore heavy clothes, far too warm for the climate. And they spoke a language the people had never heard.

Much has been said about Columbus' discovery of America on that day so long ago. But to Native Americans this "discovery" is a very strange idea. When the last Ice Age ended, 12,000 years ago, their ancestors already lived in large areas across America. Native Americans did not feel lost. How could this Spaniard say that he had found them? Why not say that they had discovered the Spaniards?

However you choose to look at it, what happened that day, 500 years ago, was of very great importance. Columbus took a group of men to the shore and claimed the island in the name of the Spanish King and Queen. He believed that he was in the Indies, so he called the people who lived there Indians. His men traded small bells, pieces of colored glass, and clothes, for

Columbus and his men setting foot on "Discovery Island"

whatever the Indians would give them. But the Indians on that first island had little that the Spaniards wanted, and so they did not stay for long.

For two days Columbus explored the island. Then he took by force six Indians to act as guides, and sailed to other islands that were near. Columbus was in the heart of the Bahama Islands, southwest of what is now Florida. The Bahamas are a group of coral islands and thousands of dangerous coral reefs, which reach across 1,000 kilometers of clear, blue sea. Columbus described the islands that he visited, and he drew a chart of the route he sailed.

Experts have identified the large islands on Columbus' charts, but they are not certain about some of the smaller ones. One island whose identity is not certain is "Discovery Island", where Columbus first walked in America. It was one of the Bahama islands, and although there are many guesses, no one knows for certain which one it was.

The search for gold

On October 14, Columbus left Discovery Island with one thing first in his mind: He wanted to find gold, jewels, spices, or other things of worth, which he could carry to Spain to show that his great enterprise had been a success. He hoped to find the rich ports of Asia, but if he could not find them, any source of gold would have made him happy. He noticed that some of the Indians on Discovery Island wore gold jewelry in their noses. They made signals that suggested their gold had come from a great island to the southwest. Columbus thought that the island of gold must be Japan.

For two weeks the fleet sailed southwest from island to island. Although they carefully checked each island for cities or gold they found nothing but beautiful landscapes, lots of trees, flowers and birds, and small villages with friendly Indians. Finally at a place along the Cuban coast, Indians told them that there was gold in the island's center. There was also a city, they said, which Columbus thought must be the great capital city of China or Japan.

Columbus sent two Spaniards and two Indians to visit the great city. They walked 40 kilometers and found the largest Indian village the Spanish had yet seen. It had 50 huts. There was not a single gold building or gold street in the place! When they returned to the ship, the most interesting thing that they reported to the Admiral was that they had seen the Indians burn dried leaves and breathe the smoke. They had seen the Indians smoke tobacco.

By now Columbus and his men were upset about their failure to find either the cities of Asia or a source of gold. They asked the Indians again and again where one could find these things, but they always said the gold was somewhere else. What Columbus did not know was that most of the gold that was worn by the Indians did not come from the Caribbean Islands, but from Mexico and Central America. Indians on the mainland traded gold to people on nearby islands. Then, these people traded with islands farther out in the Carribean. It was not until 25 years later that Ferdinand Cortez and his men landed in Mexico where they found large amounts of gold and rich natives called the Aztecs. But Columbus did not give up and he ordered his fleet to sail farther.

As the Pinta and the Nina were both faster ships than the Admiral's Santa Maria, the smaller ships often had to slow down or wait for Columbus. Early in the morning on November 22, the captain of the Pinta, however, decided to slow no more for the Santa Maria, but to sail as fast as his ship would go. Columbus was angry when he saw the Pinta sail away because he could guess the captain's reason for it: He wanted to find gold by himself. But Columbus could do nothing about it. With two ships, he slowly sailed along the Cuban coast until he reached another large island which he named Hispaniola, or "Spanish Island". Today the island is divided between the countries of Haiti and the Dominican Republic.

On Hispaniola

For 18 days, Columbus explored the rough northwestern coast of Hispaniola. He saw mountains with great forests and bays of wonderful beauty. The Spaniards even found gold, but it was not very much. As usual the Indians welcomed the Spaniards and gave them lots of food and drink. The Admiral wrote in his journal that the Indians were so friendly and peaceful that it would be easy to make them slaves.

Columbus had mixed ideas about Native Americans from the beginning. He wanted to make them Catholics, and some Indians freely chose his religion. Some became his friends and even asked to visit Spain. But other Indians fought Columbus and he was very cruel to them. His soldiers made them slaves and forced them to mine gold. Some were sent to Spain where they were sold. Queen Isabella did not like this slave trade and tried to stop it. But Spanish cruelty towards the Indians continued for many years.

Just before Christmas an Indian chief sent a messenger to Columbus with a gold present and an invitation to visit him. On December 24, the Santa Maria and the Nina raised their anchors and sailed toward the place where they were to meet the chief. In the evening the wind became calm and the ships slowed. The Admiral had not slept for two days, so an hour before midnight, he went to his room to rest. The sea was so quiet and smooth that the sailors did not watch where the ship went. When Christmas Day was only a few minutes old, the Santa Maria quietly touched on a coral reef. Too late the boy at the steering wheel made a shout.

Columbus ran onto the deck and ordered his men to drop the ship's boat. He told them to take out the anchor and drop it so that the Santa Maria would not be pushed farther onto the reef. Instead, the men in the boat were frightened and went to the Nina. By the time the Santa Maria's anchor was dropped, an hour had gone by. It was too late. Waves had pushed the ship onto the reef, and sharp coral had made holes in the bottom.

When morning came, the local Indian chief sent men and boats to carry things from the Santa Maria to shore. No one was hurt, and everything of worth had been saved. But the Santa Maria, the Admiral's ship, lay wrecked on a coral reef.

The first colony, La Navidad, is established on Hispaniola

Christmas Day, 1492, was not happy for Columbus. He had started his great enterprise with three ships. Now one was wrecked and another was gone. He had two crews with him, and only one ship. But Columbus still believed that God guided his adventure. He decided that the wreck of the Santa Maria was a sign from God, who wanted him to establish a village there on Hispaniola. This he did, and he called the village La Navidad, which is Spanish for Christmas.

Many sailors were happy to stay in Navidad. The local Indians were friendly, and there were signs of nearby gold. It would be easy to get rich in Navidad, they thought. They would simply make the Indians produce gold for them.

Two days after Christmas, some Indians came with news that the Pinta had been seen anchored in a river to the east. Columbus decided that he would soon leave Navidad to look for the Pinta and then sail home to Spain. On January 2, 1493, the local Indian chief had a great party to say goodbye to Columbus. Two days later, the Admiral sailed away in the Nina. He left behind 39 men in Navidad, with food for a year, tools to build a town, and guns.

On January 6, the Nina met the Pinta as it sailed towards Navidad. Indians had told the Pinta's men about the wreck of the Santa Maria, and they wanted to help. That night the Pinta's captain explained to the Admiral where he had been during the last few weeks. He had found no island with gold beaches, but he had explored Hispaniola and found a source of some gold in the island's center. Columbus was still angry with the man, but he welcomed the news about gold and was happy to have company on the long trip home.

Back to Spain

On January 16, the Nina and the Pinta left the island and sailed towards home. They took Indians, several birds and some gold with them. Columbus sailed northeast, to the latitude of the Azores, where he hoped to find winds from the west that would quickly blow him home.

Conditions were good for nearly a month. Then, in the middle of February, strong winds turned into terrible storms. The Nina and the Pinta were blown in different directions and lost sight of each other. Columbus was afraid that his discovery would die with him. So he wrote a summary of his journey, put it inside a wooden container, and threw it into the sea. He hoped that someone would find it, even if the Nina and the Pinta both went down.

On February 18, the Nina arrived in the Azores. The Portuguese captain of the island gave the Spaniards some trouble, but he let them go after six days. Then, between the Azores and the coast of Portugal, Columbus sailed into the most violent storms of the trip. The Nina's sails were torn into pieces by the wind before the ship finally reached the coast of Portugal, near Lisbon.

On March 4, Columbus sailed into Lisbon harbor. He bought new sails, visited the King of Portugal, and left Lisbon ten days later. About noon on March 15, 1493, the Nina sailed into the harbor in Palos, Spain. The Pinta arrived in Palos hours later. It had been blown north of the Azores during the storms. Now both ships were safe. Columbus' first great journey of discovery was over.

Chapter Four
Trouble in the New World

Columbus, the hero at the Spanish court

When Columbus returned to Spain after his first great journey, he was a hero. The King and Queen asked him to come and tell them about his adventure, and he went to see them with great ceremony. He took some of his best officers, gold, parrots, and six Indians who wore bright feathers and gold jewelry. When he saw the Queen, Columbus fell to his knees, but Isabella told her Admiral to rise and sit next to her on her right. This was the time of greatest glory for Columbus.

But not everybody admired Columbus. At the Spanish court some of the noblemen were jealous. Once at a dinner, a guest said that Columbus' journey was not important. It was true that Columbus had crossed the ocean. But if not Columbus then another man would have done so. Columbus got up and took a hard-boiled egg from a plate. He asked the noblemen at the table to make the egg stand upright. Everybody tried, but the egg kept rolling over. Finally the egg came back to Columbus. He cracked the large end: The egg stood upright easily. "Look, gentlemen," Columbus said. "Now all of you can do it. But the important person is the one who succeeds first."

Columbus spoke about his plan to establish a permanent colony on Hispaniola, and how he would mine gold, and where he would go to look for the cities of Asia. Ferdinand and Isabella were excited by his talk, and they asked him to quickly return to the Indies.

The second journey to the New World

In late September, 1493, Columbus sailed again with a fleet of 17 ships and more than 1,000 men. He took plants and animals for farms, tools to build mines and buildings, guns, and priests to make the Indians into Catholics.

Columbus solving the "egg question"

From Spain the fleet sailed to the Canary Islands. They crossed the Atlantic Ocean easily, and on November 3, Columbus was back in the Indies, this time among islands to the southeast of Hispaniola.

One day after the fleet completed its crossing of the Atlantic Ocean, the ships anchored near an island with a volcano that rose so high that its top was often lost in clouds. Columbus sent a group of men to explore the island, but the tropical forest was so heavy that they could not see the sun, and they got lost. Four more groups, each with 50 men, went to look for the first group.

For four days the Spaniards explored the island and looked for their lost friends. Brightly colored parrots flew through the dark forest, and their sounds filled the air. There were many villages, but they were empty because the Indians had run away. Inside the Indian huts, the Spaniards saw pieces of cooked meat that looked like the arms and legs of people! The Indians on that island were cannibals, members of the Carib tribe the Caribbean Sea was later named for. Caribs lived in the southern islands and attacked the more peaceful Indians to the north, who Columbus had met during his first journey. They took other Indians to be slaves and also to eat them. Had the lost Spaniards been attacked by Caribs?

Late on their fourth day on the island, the men on the ships saw a signal fire high on the side of the volcano. They hoped that the fire was made by their lost friends and asked an old Carib woman to guide them to the place. There they actually found their friends. They led them back to the ships, and the fleet sailed the next morning, away from that terrible island. But first, the Spaniards destroyed as many canoes as they could find, so the Caribs could not visit other islands for some time.

For two more weeks Columbus' ships sailed through the eastern Caribbean Sea. On the way to Hispaniola, they sailed past 20 large islands and more than 40 small islands and reefs. In late November, the fleet reached Hispaniola. As he sailed towards Navidad, Columbus looked for a good harbor where he could build a new town. In one place he sent a group of men to look around the shore. There, next to a river, they found the bodies of two dead Spaniards. This was the first suggestion of what they would find in Navidad.

Columbus was now very worried about the 39 men he had left last Christmas. Just as the sun went down, the fleet arrived near Navidad. After what had happened there to the Santa Maria Columbus would not sail through the dangerous reef in the dark, so his ships dropped anchors outside the reef. Although the sailors shot their cannons and lit signal fires, there was no answer from the shore. Navidad had been destroyed. And Columbus soon learned why.

The Spaniards in Navidad had behaved very badly, the Indians said. They had not built their town, grown food, or traded with the Indians for gold, as Columbus had expected. Instead, many of the Spaniards had formed groups and marched around the island with guns. They had taken gold and food and women. The Indians in the center of the island were not as peaceful as those around Navidad. They killed the Spaniards, attacked Navidad, and burned it to the ground.

The loss of Navidad was a serious blow to Columbus. There were 1,000 colonists on his ships but there was no colony where they could live. They would have to build everything themselves. Columbus decided to build a new town in a better place in one of the harbors he had seen along the coast.

The building of the second colony, Isabela

To return along the coast the fleet had to sail against the wind. After 25 days, they had gone only 50 kilometers, and the sailors were tired. The Admiral decided to build the new town where he was, although the place was not much better than the place where Navidad had been built. He called the new town Isabela. Isabela was closer than Navidad had been to the source of gold in the mountains, in the center of Hispaniola. Men who were sent to look for gold came back with some pieces of gold as big as pebbles. The gold made Columbus happy, but he still had many problems. He had expected fields which were planted with food in Navidad, and without them, there were too many colonists for the food supply. Most of the men were hungry, and a third of them were sick. In February, the Admiral sent 12 of his ships back to Spain, while he kept the other five in Isabela. He sent a little gold and asked the King and Queen to send in return ships that were loaded with Spanish food.

For the next six years, Columbus worked on a pair of problems. On land, he fought to develop a stable colony that would produce money. At sea, he explored new coasts and tried to find the continent of Asia. In the end, however, he did not solve either problem.

In April, 1493, Columbus left his youngest brother, Diego, in control of Isabela while he took the Nina and two other ships to look for the continent of Asia. He sailed along the southern coast of Cuba, then turned south to Jamaica, then returned to Cuba to sail farther along its southern coast. At last, the ships reached a part of the coast where the water was so shallow that the ships had to be pulled through the mud. The Admiral decided that Cuba was too big to be an island, so it must be an arm of the Asian continent. But as his men were tired and his ships leaked, he sailed back to Jamaica, and from there to Hispaniola. He became very ill on the way back and had to be carried to the shore at Isabela.

Columbus had been gone five months, and there was good news when he returned. His brother, Bartholomew, had arrived from Spain. Bartholomew was Christopher's closest assistant, and he helped his brother rule Hispaniola. He was stronger than Diego Columbus, who was much younger than his brothers. But even with the work of all three brothers Hispaniola's problems grew worse.

The colonists all wanted to collect gold, but they did not want to plant fields and build houses. The Indians were forced to produce gold, but there was not as much gold as the Spaniards expected. There was too much sickness in the colony and too little to eat. In March, 1496, Columbus ordered Bartholomew to build a new town on the southern coast. He then sailed to Spain to report to the King and Queen and to ask them for more help.

Ferdinand and Isabella were not as happy to see Columbus this time. "You always ask for more supplies," they told him, "but you never send as much gold as you promise. And when will you find China?"

The third journey to the New World

A year went by before Columbus convinced the King and Queen that they should pay for another fleet to the colony. A second year went by before the fleet was organized and ready to go. In late May, 1498, Columbus sailed for the Canaries with six ships. Three ships went from the Canaries straight to Hispaniola. The Admiral took the other three ships to explore on the way to the colony.

On his third journey to the Indies the Admiral chose a southern route. Some geographers believed there was a great continent near the equator in the western ocean, and Columbus wanted to see if they were right. He sailed south from the Canaries to Portugal's Cape Verde Islands, off the African coast. From there he sailed southwest for three days until the wind died. For a week the ships drifted in terrible heat. Then the wind returned, and the Admiral sailed west until he saw land on the last day of July.

If the wind had carried Columbus farther south before it became calm off the Cape Verde Islands, he might have landed on the coast of South America near the Amazon River. Instead, he landed on Trinidad island, about 15 kilometers off the South American coast. The ships spent several days off Trinidad. The sailors got fresh water, then they swam and had some fun. Suddenly, a huge wave, which was probably caused by a volcano under the sea, almost wrecked the ships, and Columbus decided it was time to leave Trinidad.

On shore of the South American mainland

West of Trinidad the fleet sailed into a gulf where a river from the continent released a huge amount of fresh water into the sea. Columbus explored the gulf and, on August 5, 1498, landed near an Indian village on the coast of what is now Venezuela. Men from the ships went to the shore and walked in South America for the first time. Columbus thought at the time that they had landed on another island. Later he realized that a river as big as the one he had seen must have collected water from a huge area. He wrote in his journal that they had found, not an island, but "a very great continent, until today unknown". Near this, he found Indians who got pearls from the sea. Spanish ships soon came back for more pearls.

Now it was the middle of August. As the Admiral was very sick, he ordered the fleet to go to Hispaniola. He arrived in late August two and a half years after he had left. Conditions in the colony were very serious.

Many of the colonists did not like Bartholomew's rule, and some had rebelled and taken control of part of Hispaniola with guns. It took him a year, but Columbus stopped the fighting and made peace with the rebels. He sent news of what had happened to Spain, but his troubles were not over. Colonists were still not happy, and many fought against Columbus' rule. Indians fought more and more often, too, and they were killed or died from sicknesses in very great numbers.

Finally, Ferdinand and Isabella decided to send a new governor to take control of the colony from Columbus. The new man arrived in August, 1500, but Columbus refused to accept his orders. In October, the new governor put chains on the three Columbus brothers and sent them back to Spain in the bottom of a ship.

Columbus being taken prisoner

Chapter Five
The fourth and final journey of Columbus

No longer a hero

Between the spring of 1493 and the autumn of 1500 the reputation of Columbus dropped as low as it could go. He was a great hero in Spain after his first journey of discovery. He returned from his third journey in chains like a criminal.

Columbus waited to hear from the King and Queen for six weeks after he returned. At last, in early December, 1500, they released him from his chains and asked him to visit them. Columbus had failed as a governor, but Queen Isabella was still kind to him. She gave back his money and titles, but not his power to rule Hispaniola. He asked the King and Queen to let him return to the colony. For a year they said no. Conditions had changed. Columbus was not the only man who explored for Spain.

In 1499 and 1500, two men who had earlier sailed with Columbus commanded their own fleets to the new lands. They collected pearls from west of Trinidad, where Columbus had explored in 1498. They also explored the coast of South America, at least as far south as the Amazon River. On the first of these two journeys there was another man from Genoa, like Columbus. His name was Amerigo Vespucci. The new world of America was later named after him.

By 1500, England and Portugal were interested in lands across the western sea. In 1497, John Cabot, another explorer who was born in Genoa, sailed from England to Newfoundland, the Vinland of the Vikings. He may have reached the continent of North America. He sailed again the next year, but no one knows what happened on that trip. Probably Cabot's ship went down.

A Portuguese ship, which was commanded by Vasco da Gama, finally sailed around Africa to India and back. The journey took two years and ended in 1499. The next year a Portuguese fleet on the way to India sailed far to the west of Africa and touched what is now Brazil.

The fourth journey to the New World

There was so much competition to explore new lands and new routes to Asia that Ferdinand and Isabella were forced to continue to develop Hispaniola. In early 1502 they sent the biggest fleet yet to their colony, 32 ships with 2,500 sailors and colonists. The King and Queen also said Columbus could return to look again for a route to Asia. They told him not to go to Hispaniola, unless he had to stop on his way back to Spain.

In May, 1502, Columbus sailed from Spain with four ships and 150 men. Bartholomew, his brother, was with him, and so was Ferdinand, his youngest son, who was 13 years old. The fleet arrived in the New World in June, 1502, and sailed straight to Hispaniola, against the orders of the King and Queen. Columbus recognized from the clouds and waves that a terrible hurricane was about to hit the island. A fleet of 30 ships was ready to go to Spain, and Columbus told the new governor of the island to hold the fleet until after the storm. He also asked if he could bring his four ships into the harbor in Santo Domingo, the capital city Bartholomew had established.

The governor laughed at Columbus and would not let him into the harbor. Then he sent the fleet out, just before the hurricane hit. Five ships in the fleet survived, but 25 were destroyed. Columbus' ships also survived in a harbor near Santo Domingo.

After the hurricane the Admiral sailed west with his fleet to the coast of Central America, then he turned and sailed southeast along the coast. Columbus still believed that the continent of Asia was near. If only he could find the right route through all the islands and land, he thought, then he could sail to the rich ports of Asia!

On the gold coast of Panama

The fleet explored the Central American coast for months. Men went to the shore in many places to look for gold, trade with the Indians, and to ask them about China. They found gold along part of the coast of what is now Panama. But there were no good harbors there, so they sailed on. In late autumn and winter heavy rain made it difficult to sail. The sailors were very tired by early December, so Columbus decided to go back to collect some of the gold he had found earlier.

Two days before Christmas, 1502, Columbus' ships stopped in the harbor that is now the entrance to the Panama Canal. They were as close to the Pacific Ocean as they would ever come. If Columbus had only known, he could have borrowed canoes from the Indians and sent some men up the river that entered that harbor. They could have gone up the river as far as their canoes would go, and there, they would have been only 20 kilometers by land from the Pacific Ocean. Of course, Columbus did not look for a land route because he wanted a sea route to China. And there was no sea route from the Caribbean Sea into the Pacific Ocean — not until the Panama Canal was built four centuries later.

In early 1503, Columbus reached the gold coast of Panama. For three months, his men collected gold and traded with the Indians. There was so much gold that he decided to build a small camp and leave some men there with one of the ships. But some of the men used guns to steal things from the Indians. There were more and more fights between Spaniards and Indians.

Columbus remembered what had happened at Navidad, and he decided not to build a camp in Panama. But the ship he had planned to leave had become stuck in shallow water, and the men could not free it. With only three ships the Admiral left the gold coast of Panama.

The men and ships of Columbus had been at sea for a year, and they needed help. Columbus suffered from a tropical disease.

There was little food left, and all three ships leaked. One leaked so much that it soon had to be left behind. After that there were two ships to carry four tired crews to Hispaniola, 1,000 kilometers away.

Marooned on Jamaica

On May 1, the damaged ships sailed north. Twelve days later they reached the coast of Cuba. They were almost out of food, and the ships leaked more every day. Then a violent storm hit, and it lasted for six days. When his ships could sail again, Columbus followed the coast of Cuba towards Hispaniola.

In early June, Columbus decided to leave the coast and jump across the last 300 kilometers of open sea. The ships sailed slowly because the wind was against them. When they were still 150 kilometers from Hispaniola, they were about to sink. Columbus turned and sailed with the wind to Jamaica, where he ordered the ships to sail onto a white sand beach.

Columbus was marooned on Jamaica with 115 men. They traded with the Indians for food. In August one brave Spaniard tried to cross from Jamaica to Hispaniola in an Indian canoe. On his second try he made it across 175 kilometers of water to Hispaniola! He told the governor that Columbus was marooned on Jamaica. But the governor did not want Columbus on his island, so he refused to send a ship to get him!

On Jamaica conditions were not happy. The Spaniards often fought against each other. Many men were sick. In early 1504, food supplies were almost gone when Columbus noticed in a book that an eclipse of the moon was about to happen. He told the Indians that he would put out the moon and terrible things would happen to them and their country if they did not bring more food. After the eclipse the Spaniards had lots to eat for a while.

In March, the governor of Hispaniola sent a ship to see if Columbus was alive. He sent some wine and meat, but ordered the ship not to bring anyone back to the colony. Three months later another ship arrived to rescue the marooned men. A hundred survivors reached the colony in August. They had been marooned for a year.

Back in Spain

The fourth great adventure of Columbus ended in Spain in early November 1504. Three weeks later Queen Isabella died. The Admiral was so sick that he could not travel to her funeral. After six months he was healthy enough to visit the King. He asked Ferdinand to let him rule Hispaniola again, but the King would not agree. Columbus then asked him to make his older son, Diego, governor. Later, Diego was governor, but not while Columbus was alive.

A man in his fifties is not an old man today, but life was very hard 500 years ago. Columbus felt sick and old during the last years of his life. And he was disappointed that people did not recognize how much he had done.

On May 21, 1506, Christopher Columbus quietly died in Spain. He was 54 years old. But our story of the man who discovered America does not end there. He made one final journey across the sea. In 1542, his body was sent by ship to Hispaniola, where he was buried in the cathedral of Santa Domingo, next to his son, Diego.

***

In the 500 years since Columbus landed in America, the world has changed more than anyone could have imagined. Columbus was brave enough and stubborn enough to open a door in history. Spain hurried through that door, then Portugal, England, France, and most of the rest of Europe. But while Columbus opened the door, he never really understood what was on the other side.

Columbus probably always believed that his new lands were a part of Asia. Sixteen years after he died, Spanish ships that were commanded by Ferdinand Magellan sailed around the world. Magellan was killed during the journey, but before he died, he showed that North and South America were new continents between Europe and Asia. By the time Magellan was killed, Spaniards had already defeated the Aztecs of Mexico. Thousands of Indians all through Central America and the Caribbean Sea were killed in battle. Millions more had died from diseases that were unknown to them but that had been carried from Europe. A million Indians lived on Hispaniola when Columbus landed there just before Christmas in 1492. Forty years later only about 10,000 Indians had survived.

Today, we see how terribly important these events were, but this was not understood in the early sixteenth century. Even Columbus' death was noticed by few people in Spain. And he had so many enemies that some people who noticed it did not care. One year later, when the German geographer, Martin Waldseemüller, produced a new map of the world, he suggested that Spain's new lands be named after Amerigo Vespucci, not after Columbus. Columbus was a more important explorer, but the stories Vespucci wrote about his adventures were so popular that people often forgot about Columbus.

Even in America, Columbus' achievement was little celebrated for the first three centuries. But that had changed by October 12, 1892, the 400th anniversary of the day Columbus landed in America. There were huge celebrations in America that day, and October 12 became a permanent national holiday, Columbus Day.

Today, people argue about Columbus as they did in his own time. Was he a great man? The Vikings discovered America long before Columbus. To many Native Americans Columbus Day is a sad day, and not a day to celebrate. Columbus brought death and destruction to them.

The truth is that Columbus was a man of many faces. And he was a man of his own time, not of ours. His was a time of bravery and of slavery, of discovery and of mistakes.
The three small ships of Columbus carried things both horrible and wonderful to America and back again. The Nina, the Pinta, and the Santa Maria carried the future.

Vocabulary

A **about:** (to) **be about to do sth.** im Begriff sein, etwas zu tun
achievement [ə'tʃi:vmənt] Leistung
admiral ['ædmərəl] Admiral/in
(to) **admire** [əd'maɪə] bewundern
after all [ɑ:ftər‿'ɔ:l] schließlich, immerhin
ahead [ə'hed] vorn
Arab ['ærəb] Araber/in; arabisch

B (to) **be about to do sth.** im Begriff sein, etwas zu tun
(to) **be supposed to do sth.** [sə'pəʊst] etwas tun sollen
beyond [bɪ'jɒnd] über ... hinaus, jenseits
blow [bləʊ] Schlag
bottom ['bɒtm] Boden
bravery ['breɪvrɪ] Tapferkeit
(to) **breathe** [bri:ð] atmen
by now mittlerweile, inzwischen

C **Canaries, Canary Islands** [kə'neərɪz, kə'neərɪ] Kanaren, kanarische Inseln
cannibal ['kænɪbl] Kannibale, Kannibalin
cannon ['kænən] (Bord-)Kanone
Carib ['kærɪb] Karibe, Karibin
Caribbean [kærə'bi:ən] karibisch; Karibik
carved [kɑ:vd] geschnitzt
Catholic ['kæθlɪk] Katholik/in; katholisch
chain [tʃeɪn] Kette, Fessel
chart [tʃɑ:t] Seekarte
chief [tʃi:f] Häuptling
Christian ['krɪstʃn] Christ/in; christlich
(to) **claim** [kleɪm] Anspruch erheben auf
(to) **clear** [klɪə] *hier:* sich verziehen

(to) **command** [kə'mɑːnd] das Kommando führen, den Befehl haben
company ['kʌmpənɪ] Begleitung
complaint [kəm'pleɪnt] Klage, Beschwerde
coral ['kɒrəl] Koralle
course [kɔːs] Kurs
(to) **crack** [kræk] aufschlagen
crew [kruː] Besatzung, Mannschaft
cruelty ['krʊəltɪ] Grausamkeit
Cuba ['kjuːbə] Kuba
Cuban ['kjuːbn] Kubaner/in; kubanisch

D **disappointment** [dɪsə'pɔɪntmənt] Enttäuschung
(to) **discourage** [dɪs'kʌrɪdʒ] entmutigen
(to) **discover** [dɪ'skʌvə] entdecken
discovery [dɪ'skʌvərɪ] Entdeckung
disease [dɪ'ziːz] Krankheit
distant ['dɪstənt] entfernt
(to) **drop** [drɒp] *hier:* sich legen

E **eclipse** [ɪ'klɪps] *hier:* Mondfinsternis
empire ['empaɪə] Reich
enterprise ['entəpraɪz] Unternehmen, Unternehmung
equator [ɪ'kweɪtə] Äquator
(to) **explore** [ɪk'splɔː] (die Gegend) erforschen

F **failure** ['feɪljə] Versagen; Mißerfolg
(to) **fall in love with** sich verlieben in
final['faɪnl] letzte(r, s)
fleet [fliːt] Flotte
(to) **float** [fləʊt] (im Wasser) treiben
for [fɔː] denn
force: by force [fɔːs] mit Gewalt
(to) **free** [friː] befreien

(to) **frighten** ['fraɪtn] erschrecken
funeral ['fju:nərəl] Begräbnis

G **geographer** [dʒɪ'ɒgrəfə] Geograph/in
(to) **get lost, got lost, got lost** sich verirren
(to) **give birth to** [bɜ:θ] gebären, zur Welt bringen
glory ['glɔ:rɪ] Ruhm
good luck [lʌk] Glück
got lost → (to) **get lost**
governor ['gʌvnə] Gouverneur/in, Statthalter/in
grape [greɪp] Weintraube
Greeks of old die alten Griechen
Greenland ['gri:nlənd] Grönland
guard [gɑ:d] (be)schützen, wachen über
(to) **guess** [ges] Vermutung, Annahme
(to) **guide** [gaɪd] lenken, leiten

H **hole** [həʊl] Loch
however *hier:* wie auch immer
hurricane ['hʌrɪkn] Wirbelsturm, Orkan

I **Ice Age** ['--] Eiszeit
Iceland ['aɪslənd] Island
(to) **identify** [aɪ'dentifaɪ] identifizieren
if he had only known, ... wenn er nur gewußt hätte
importance [ɪm'pɔ:təns] Bedeutung, Wichtigkeit
in addition [ə'dɪʃn] außerdem
Indies ['ɪndɪz] Ostindien (*alter Name für Vorder- und Hinterindien*)

J **jealous** ['dʒeləs] neidisch
jewelry ['dʒu:əlrɪ] Schmuck
journal ['dʒɜ:nl] Tagebuch
journey ['dʒɜ:nɪ] Reise

K (to) **keep ties** [taɪz] die Verbindung halten

L **latitude: in the latitude of** ['lætɪtju:d] *hier:* auf der Höhe, in der Gegend von

(to) **leak** [li:k] lecken, leck sein

(to) **light, lit, lit** [laɪt, lɪt, lɪt] anzünden

lit → (to) **light**

loss [lɒs] Verlust

M **mainland** ['meɪnlənd] Festland

(to) **make sth./sb. do sth.** etwas/jn. veranlassen, etwas zu tun

(to) **march around** [mɑ:tʃ] umherziehen

(to) **maroon** [mə'ru:n] von der (Außen-)Welt abgeschnitten sein

Mediterranean Sea [medɪtəreɪnɪən 'si:] Mittelmeer

(to) **mine** [maɪn] abbauen

Muslim ['mʊzləm] Moslem; moslemisch

N (to) **name** [neɪm] nennen

nearby [nɪə'baɪ] nahegelegen

nobleman, noblemen ['nəʊblmən, 'nəʊblmən] Adliger, Edelmann

noon [nu:n] Mittag

O **off** [ɒf] weg von; (weiter) entfernt

on behalf [bɪ'hɑ:f] im Auftrag von

(to) **order** ['ɔ:də] befehlen, anordnen

out of: (to) **be out of sth.** etwas nicht mehr haben

P **palm tree** ['pɑ:m tri:] Palme

pearl [pɜ:l] Perle

pebble ['pebl] Kiesel(stein)

people ['pi:pl] *hier:* Volk

(to) **plant** [plɑ:nt] (be)pflanzen

Portuguese [pɔ:tʃʊ'gi:z] Portugiese, Portugiesin; portugiesisch
priest [pri:st] Priester/in

R (to) **raise one's anchor** [reɪz, 'æŋkə] den Anker einholen/lichten
(to) **rebel** [rɪ'bel] rebellieren, sich auflehnen
reef [ri:f] Riff
reputation [repjʊ'teɪʃn] Ruf
(to) **rescue** ['reskju:] retten
(to) **roll over** [rəʊl] sich herumdrehen
(to) **rule** [ru:l] regieren, herrschen über

S **sailing ship** Segelschiff
search [sɜ:tʃ] Suche
shallow ['ʃæləʊ] flach, seicht
shore [ʃɔ:] Strand, Küste
single: not a single one ['sɪŋgl] kein(e) einzige(r,s)
(to) **slow down** [sləʊ] (die Geschwindigkeit) verlangsamen
smooth [smu:ð] glatt
(to) **solve** [sɒlv] lösen
source [sɔ:s] Quelle
spice [spaɪs] Gewürz
stable [steɪbl] stabil, dauerhaft
stubborn ['stʌbən] eigensinnig, dickköpfig
stuck: (to) **become stuck** [stʌk] steckenbleiben
(to) **suggest that sth. be done** [sə'dʒest] vorschlagen, daß etwas getan wird
superstition [su:pə'stɪʃn] Aberglaube
supplies [sə'plaɪz] Vorrat, Proviant
supposed: (to) **be supposed to do sth.** [sə'pəʊst] etwas tun sollen
surviver [sə'vaɪvə] Überlebende/r
(to) **tear, tore, torn** [teə, tɔ:, tɔ:n] (zer)reißen

T **tip** [tɪp] Spitze
torn → (to) **tear**
trade [treɪd] Handel
(to) **trade** [treɪd] Handel treiben; (aus)tauschen
trade wind ['--] Passatwind
tragic [trædʒɪk] tragisch
tropical ['trɒpɪkl] tropisch
Turkey ['tɜːkɪ] Türkei

U **underneath** [ʌndə'niːθ] *hier:* auf der Unterseite
unless [ən'les] wenn ... nicht
upright ['ʌpraɪt] aufrecht, senkrecht

V **Viking** ['vaɪkɪŋ] Wikinger/in; Wikinger-
volcano, volcanoes [vɒl'keɪnəʊ/z] Vulkan

W (to) **wait for sb. to do sth.** darauf warten, daß jd. etwas tut
weaver ['wiːvə] Weber/in
(to) **welcome** ['welkəm] willkommen heißen
westward ['westwəd] nach Westen, westwärts
wooden ['wʊdn] aus Holz
would: he would have done er würde getan haben
wrecked [rekt] zerstört

Y **yet** [jet] *hier:* bisher

Names

Family names

Cabot ['kæbət]
Columbus [kə'lʌmbəs]
Cortez ['kɔːtez]
da Gama [də 'gɑːmə]

Erickson ['erɪksn]
Magellan [mə'gelən]
Vespucci [ve'spu:tʃɪ]

Girls/women

Isabella [ɪzə'belə]

Boys/men

Amerigo [ɑ:mə'ri:gəʊ]
Bartholomew [bɑ:'θɒləmju:]
Christopher ['krɪstəfə]
Diego [dɪ'eɪgəʊ]
Ferdinand ['fɜ:dɪnænd]
Leif [li:f]
Vasco ['væskəʊ]

Place names

Amazon ['æməzn]
Azores [ə'zɔ:z]
Bahama(s) [bə'hɑ:mə(z)]
Cape Verde Islands [keɪp 'vɜ:d]
Cuba ['kju:bə]
Dominican Republic [də'mɪnɪkn]
Genoa ['dʒenəʊə]
Haiti ['heɪtɪ]
Hispaniola [hɪspænɪ'əʊlə]
Isabela [ɪzə'belə]
Jamaica [dʒə'meɪkə]
La Navidad [lɑ: nʌvɪ'dɑ:d]
Lisbon ['lɪzbən]
Newfoundland ['nju:fənlənd]
Nuremberg ['njʊərəmbɜ:g]

Palos ['pɑːləʊs]
Panama ['pænəmɑː]
Portugal ['pɔːtʃʊgəl]
Santo Domingo ['sæntəʊ də'mɪŋgəʊ]
Tenerife [tenə'riːf]
Trinidad ['trɪnɪdæd]
Venezuela [venə'zweɪlə]
Vinland ['vɪnlənd]

Others
Aztec(s) ['æztek(s)]
Nina ['niːnə]
Santa Maria ['sæntə mə'riːə]

Bildquellen

Alle Fotos einschließlich Titel von: Archiv für Kunst und Geschichte, Berlin.
Titel: Porträt von Kolumbus von Veit Froer, um 1860, Stahlstich nach zeitgenössischem Bildnis; S. 12: „Kolumbus bricht zur ersten Entdeckungsfahrt auf", aus: Honorius Philoponus, *Nova typis transacta navigatio novi orbis Indiae Occidentalis*, Venedig 1621, Kupferstich; S. 19: „Columbus betritt die neue Welt" von Bernhard Rode, aus: J.M. Schröckh, *Weltgeschichte für Kinder*, Leipzig 1779–84, Radierung; S. 26: „Das Ei des Kolumbus", um 1880, Holzstich nach den Gemälden von Reiffenstein; S. 32: „Columbus wirdt mit seinem Bruder Bartholomeo gefänglich in Hispanien geschickt" von Theodor de Bry, aus: H. Benzoni, *America pars quarta*, Frankfurt 1594, Kupferstich

Columbus' first and second voyages

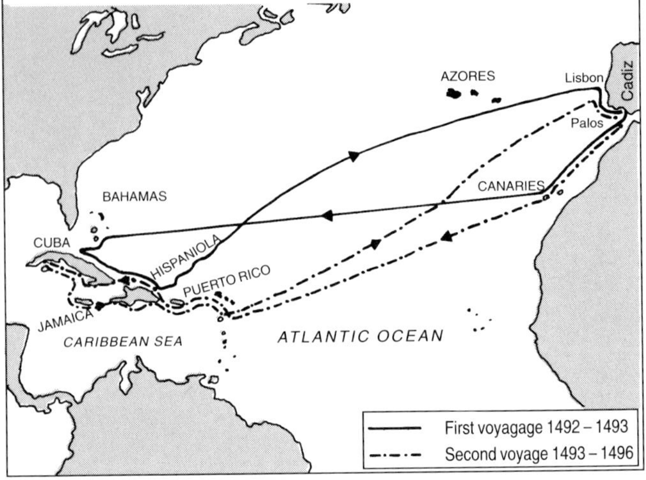

Columbus' third and fourth voyages

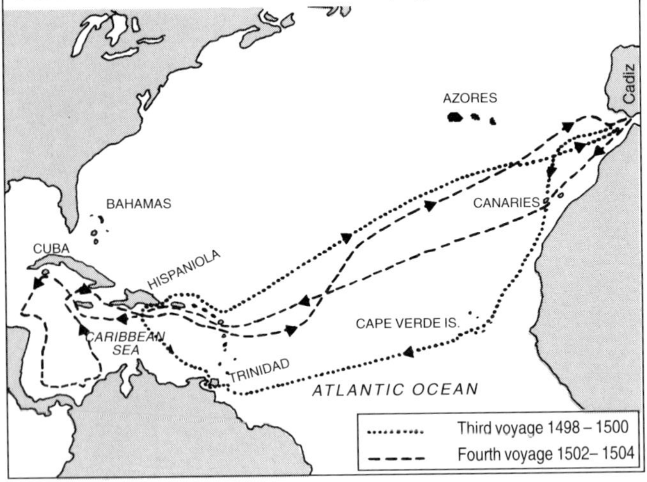